GW00725529

Test your

Verbal
Reasoning

GENE CROZIER

Series editors: GARETH LEWIS & GENE CROZIER

Hodder & Stoughton

A MEMBER OF THE HODDER HEADLINE GROUP

The Institute of Management (IM) is the leading
organisation for professional management. Its purpose is
to promote the art and science of management in every
sector and at every level, through research, education,
training and development, and representation of
members' views on management issues.

This series is commissioned by IM Enterprises Limited,
a subsidiary of the Institute of Management, providing
commercial services.

Management House,
Cottingham Road,
Corby,
Northants NN17 1TT
Tel: 01536 204222;
Fax: 01536 201651
Website: http://www.inst-mgt.org.uk

Registered in England no 3834492
Registered office: 2 Savoy Court, Strand,
London WC2R 0EZ

Orders: please contact Bookpoint Ltd, 39 Milton Park, Abingdon, Oxon OX14
4TD. Telephone: (44) 01235 400414, Fax: (44) 01235 400454. Lines are open from
9.00 – 6.00, Monday to Saturday, with a 24 hour message answering service.
Email address: orders@bookpoint.co.uk

British Library Cataloguing in Publication Data
A catalogue record for this title is available from The British Library

ISBN 0 340 789530

First published 2000
Impression number   10 9 8 7 6 5 4 3 2 1
Year   2004 2003 2002 2001 2000

Copyright © 2000 Gene Crozier

Typeset by Fakenham Photosetting Limited, Fakenham, Norfolk.
Printed in Great Britain for Hodder & Stoughton Education, a division of
Hodder Headline Plc, 338 Euston Road, London NW1 3BH by Cox & Wyman
Ltd, Reading, Berkshire.

Contents

Introduction

The 'Test Yourself' series covers a wide range of skills, competencies, capabilities and styles that contribute to our uniqueness as individuals and our performance in the workplace. Some of these qualities can be measured by objective tests that we call psychometric tests. Others are assessed using a variety of other methods.

The use of psychometric or psychological tests has grown enormously in the last few decades – so much so that if you apply for a job in a medium to large organisation, the chances are three to one that you will be required to take a psychometric test at some stage during the selection process. The tests used fall into two major groups. One of these groups focuses on aspects of typical performance and measures aspects of our preferences, style and developed habits. Tests of personality fall into this category. The other group focuses on aspects of maximum performance. These are the tests of aptitude and ability, which include the tests of verbal reasoning that we cover in this book. Verbal reasoning tests aim to measure an individual's ability to use language and to comprehend the written word. In the workplace this ability is linked to tasks that involve oral and written communication.

This group of tests is important for a number of reasons:

- They represent a wide range of skills and abilities that can be tested
- Most assessment processes involve one test of aptitude or ability
- People fear these tests more than any others

This last point is quite important. We fear these tests because they seek to measure aspects of our abilities and talents that other people judge us by and by which we judge ourselves. Often this fear is also based on a lack of knowledge of how such tests are designed and what they measure.

This book is designed to explain and reassure. We will set out what it is exactly that these tests measure, and how this is achieved. We will describe some of the most common tests and will give you a chance to 'have a go' to get a good idea of your own abilities in this area. Finally, we will explain how these tests fit in with the repertoire of other kinds of test, and what use is made of the information.

The chapters in this book take the following sequence:

- **The background**: the nature of psychometric tests.
- **The nature of verbal reasoning**: the underlying theory behind general aptitude and ability testing.
- **Verbal reasoning tests**: details of some of the main types of question and test used to assess verbal reasoning.
- **Preparing for tests**: advice on how to do well in tests.
- **Test yourself**: a self-administered verbal reasoning test.
- **Where to go next**: developing your skills.

The background

In this first chapter we shall examine the background to verbal reasoning testing, set against the context of general psychometric testing. That this is increasingly seen as important is witnessed by the substantial growth in the use of general aptitude or reasoning testing in recent times.

To do this we will consider:

- What are psychometric tests?
- What makes a test psychometric?
- How tests are designed.
- How tests are used.

What are psychometric tests?

One of the most important changes in society over the last fifty years has been the growing impact of psychology on our lives. In every walk of life, the importance of an individual's personal qualities, attitudes, skills and experience in influencing the way they interact with others is increasingly recognised. We all know that successful marketing campaigns are designed to press the right 'psychological' buttons in the population and we are much more open to discussing the role of personality in the workplace.

Matching this growth, there has also been an explosion in the use of psychological or psychometric tests. There are now literally hundreds of publishing houses selling thousands of psychometric tests in every shape and form. Just one of these volumes sells millions of copies every year, so testing is big business. People often equate 'psychometric' or 'psychological' tests with 'personality' tests, but in fact psychometric tests include a much wider range of tests than personality tests. So, what is the difference between the two and how do we recognise them?

Finding a good definition of a psychometric test is not that easy. The British Psychological Society offers the following:

'an instrument designed to produce a quantitative assessment of some psychological attribute or attributes.'

'Some psychological attribute' gives us a lot of freedom to interpret the phrase, but certainly doesn't shed too much light on the subject!

Put in a different way, it is a device or test (commonly, but not necessarily, a questionnaire) that provides measurements of any aspect of our psychology, *i.e.* thinking or behaviour that can be measured. In general, they tend to relate to two distinct (but overlapping) kinds of performance – maximum and habitual performance.

Maximum performance
Maximum performance tests measure our potential or ability to do certain things. They include tests of intelligence, aptitude or ability, including the verbal reasoning tests covered by this book. Typically these tests:

- Have right or wrong answers
- Measure ability or achievement under strict conditions
- Have a time limit
- Involve a level of difficulty so that performance can be compared person to person

In general, there are three classes of aptitude or ability tests:

1. **Objective ability tests** – which test mental abilities, or more specific occupational abilities. Verbal reasoning tests fall into this group.
2. **Achievement or attainment tests** – which measure acquired skills such as reading, clerical coding and basic operator skills.
3. **Performance tests** – developed for many craft and technical jobs; these often include standardised work sample tests (e.g. typing tests). As well as current ability, they can also measure the ability to learn in real work situations.

Habitual performance
Habitual performance (sometimes called *typical performance)* tests measure characteristic ways of behaving or thinking. They can also involve measurement of how we perceive the world, our attitudes, values and interests.

Typically, they:

- are self-descriptive
- indicate most typical behaviour or preferences
- don't involve right or wrong answers.

These are the tests that are often referred to as psychological tests or personality tests.

What makes a test psychometric?

Clearly, as the name implies, this has something to do with measurement. It is primarily the fact that we measure and quantify attributes which distinguishes psychometric testing from subjective judgement. However, developing a test is a whole process and involves a number of separate components.

There are therefore a number of criteria that enable us to classify a test as psychometric. These include:

- It is designed using psychometric principles
- It is administered in a standardised way
- It is scored and interpreted in a standardised way.

Let us examine these three criteria more closely.

How are tests designed?

A lot of work goes into designing and evaluating psychometric tests. Typically, test designers produce a very large number of questions in the early stages of test design and then reduce and refine the questions by subjecting them to an extensive set of statistical tests. This is the most important stage of test design because it needs to show that the test actually measures what it says it does and reliably. It is also the most technical part of test construction, and often ignored by test users, on the basis that the hard work and the arithmetic has been done by the test constructor. This is a pity because not all tests are as impressive in achieving their aims as the publishers would like everyone to think.

Here we will just provide brief overview of the approach, which involves two main concepts:

- Validity
- Reliability

Validity

A test is valid if it measures what it says it measures. This is a simple starting point, but validity can be a complex topic. There are a number of facets to it, and thus a number of different ways of describing, measuring and demonstrating validity.

The most important are :

Face validity – this is the extent to which the test appears to the user to test the attribute in question. Its main value is in gaining co-operation from test takers. For a verbal reasoning test, face validity would be the degree to which you felt the test was assessing your use of language (e.g. spelling, grammar, vocabulary) and ability to draw conclusions from pieces of text.

Construct validity – the degree to which the test fully describes the attribute being measured. A verbal reasoning test is said to high construct validity if it matches our understanding of the underlying nature of verbal reasoning ability.

Content validity – answers the question 'does this test measure all aspects of the attribute in question?', i.e. for a verbal reasoning test does it use all the recognised elements in verbal reasoning?

Criterion-related validity – whether the test can predict something important such as academic or job performance. This of course justifies the use of the test for clinical, educational or occupational use. Use of a verbal reasoning test to select applicants for particular jobs will be done on the basis that research has shown that high performers in the test tend to do well in the job concerned.

Reliability

Reliability has two distinct meanings. A test is reliable if it is consistent, that is, if its various parts are measuring the same thing.

A good test should also provide the same score for each subject when it is re-tested. This is called test–retest reliability.

Reliability is also important as it in turn effects the validity, i.e. in practice, valid tests are consistent.

Administering tests

The results of tests are meaningful and reliable only if everyone takes the test under the same conditions. This can be illustrated by a very simple example. Suppose you want to test a group of people using an aptitude test for verbal reasoning. You could just hand the test out and ask people to return it in the next few days. However, there would be some major disadvantages to using this approach:

- They might have different interpretations of the instructions and might fill in the questionnaire incorrectly
- They might ask their friends about the answers or even get them to take the test
- They would be doing the test under different conditions
- They would take differing amounts of time to do the test.

Clearly, if we then used the results to make decisions, such as selecting people for jobs or deciding their level of pay, this method would turn out to be most unfair. To make any test fair and reliable therefore, we must ensure that everybody experiences the same conditions. In fact, test suppliers usually supply a user manual which describes the test administration in some detail, including the actual script to be spoken. This increases the impression of 'sitting an examination' amongst test-takers, but is there to ensure consistency and fairness.

Scoring and interpreting tests
A perfect test should accurately assess the skill in question (validity) and should produce the same results (reliability) when used on the same person. Of course no such test exists, but a good test should minimise the potential for variation and provide definite guidance on the skills of the test-taker. This is why fixed choice or multiple questionnaires are favoured by test designers. Test producers usually provide scoring keys or computerised versions of the test with automatic scoring built into the software to ensure that the possibility of mistakes in scoring is minimised. Test producers also provide technical manuals and often computerised report-generating software to ensure that the interpretation of test results is as consistent as possible.

Test results must also be compared to the rest of the population or a specific group of people to have any meaning. The standardisation of scores against the standards found in part or all of the general population (the so-called norms) is a topic that we shall return to in Chapter 5.

Why aptitude tests are used by organisations

One of the main reasons why there has been such a growth
in the use of psychometric tests is that organisational
priorities have been changing. In the information age and
the knowledge economy, increasing importance is being
placed on the skills, capabilities and knowledge of
employees. Indeed, more and more organisations are
recognising that the intellectual capital of their employees is
their most important asset. Not only do they need to
identify these skills more accurately, but they also need to
know how to develop and exploit them effectively.
Increased mobility in the job market, linked to a greater
awareness of the cost of making the wrong appointment,
has led to a search for more 'intelligent' tools to assess
people for recruitment purposes. There has also been an
increased awareness of human resource management issues
in quality frameworks, such as the UK's *Investors In People*
initiative. Also, greater attention has been paid to
assessment through the widespread development of
performance management schemes.

Psychometric tests have been able to provide some answers
to these issues. Testing itself has become more sophisticated
with many more tests and suppliers of tests within the
market. Psychometric testing is increasingly being applied
in many human resource management functions. These
include:

- Selection and recruitment
- Training needs analysis
- Training and development

- Team development
- Change and culture initiatives
- Performance management
- Career counselling

Selection and recruitment

One of the key areas of growth in the use of psychometric tests in organisations has been in selection and recruitment. If you apply for a job in a larger organisation or use a selection and recruitment agency for career development, then you can expect to be required to take some form of test and probably both for aptitude and ability as well as personality. Why is this so? Well, for most of our working lives, the curriculum vitae along with the interview has been the stock in trade procedure for selection. Yet there is a wealth of evidence that it is flawed. It has been shown, for example, that:

- Interviewers make up their mind about a candidate from first impressions and then seek to justify that judgement
- Judgements are often based on less than rational grounds like appearance, gender, accent etc.
- Few interviewers have appropriate training or skills for the job
- Even a well conducted interview is only 25% more effective than choosing someone by sticking a pin in a list of candidates (BPS).

In practice therefore, selection decisions are too often based on a collection of first impressions, negative information, self delusion on the part of interviewers and stereotyping. All of these limitations stem from the fact that interviewers base their decisions on data that is almost entirely subjective.

Recognition that many selection processes are flawed has led HR professionals to identify more rational and effective ways to carry out selection. One good incentive for this is to avoid the cost of getting it wrong. Even for a middle manager, a poor appointment can cost upwards of £100,000 when the indirect as well as the direct costs are taken into account. This means quite clearly that it is significantly cheaper to do it right the first time and every time, even if the costs of selection are higher. Psychometric testing has an important role to play in good selection procedures and can greatly increase the chances of success.

Aptitude and ability tests can be linked to the *job description*, which has been designed though a comprehensive job analysis. Personality questionnaires can then provide insight into the degree of fit between an individual and the *person specification* set out in the job spec.

Other applications
As mentioned above, aptitude and ability tests are not only used for the purposes of recruitment and selection. They can also help to enhance a whole range of other human resource management functions.

Here are just a few.

1. Career progression
   Organisations are becoming much more intelligent in identifying the abilities that help them to promote people

to a level of maximum effectiveness. Historically, people were often promoted on the basis of their success in old roles, not necessarily on the skills and abilities required in future roles. They also had to work their way through the system. Many organisations now need to maximise their use of staff and to build in career progression in order to retain skilled expertise. The use of psychometric tests to build up a comprehensive profile of an individual to identify future possibilities is becoming a common practice in larger organisations.

In these situations, testing does not (or should not) replace the need for other data to be taken into consideration. Information about experience, performance and qualifications still has a role to play, but testing can provide an extra source of information that may not be obvious from these other sources. It can provide detailed and standardised data in relation to specific skills (such as the ability to manipulate complex data, or to handle numerical data) or to deeper, underlying aptitudes.

2. Advisory and career counselling processes
   In many ways, this is a similar story to that above. Testing can help to build a rich picture of strengths and weaknesses in the context of career counselling. Whether this is done internally within an organisation, or by some outside agency, it tends to happen at a watershed in a person's career. By having a wider range of information, the choices can be evaluated more objectively.

3. Assessment for development
   There has been a substantial growth in recent years in the use of assessment to support individual and team development activities. This has also resulted in a

subtle shift away from testing by organisations for their own benefit towards assessment done in partnership with the individuals involved. Although aptitude and ability tests can play a part in such processes, tests of typical performance such as personality tests, team role profiles and career preferences are generally more popular here.

The role of verbal reasoning and other aptitude tests
Information about aptitude and ability is one of the ways that organisations can satisfy the requirement of being more objective and more accurate in their assessment of individuals, as described above. Verbal reasoning tests have long featured in the selection procedures for some public sector organisations like the Police and the Civil Service. The reason for this is fairly clear. Police officers need to function effectively in the English language on a daily basis; civil servants need to be able to read and write reports effectively.

If we think of verbal reasoning as a measure of our 'word power' and ability to communicate effectively, then we can identify many jobs where oral and written skills are required. We would expect writers, scientists, researchers, actors, teachers, administrators, lawyers and librarians to all possess these skills.

But there are also many jobs where the links may be less obvious. Let's examine a few typical roles. As we discussed above, the best way of identifying the requirements for a job is first to draw up a description of the job (the job description) and then to identify the range of personal skills and qualities required by the postholder (the person spec).

Job	Receptionist	Service Engineer	Telephone Sales Person
Key Tasks	Greet visitors and look after them in reception area Contact members of staff Manage the visitors pass system Operate the switchboard Receive deliveries and organise mail	Organise a repair visits rota Repair equipment Sell replacement equipment Order spare parts Manage the team	Identify potential customers Sell products Produce purchase orders

Each of these jobs in turn requires different skills, knowledge and experience, some of which are directly dictated by the job itself and the work involved. Here are a few obvious skills for each of these jobs:

Job	Receptionist	Service Engineer	Telephone Sales Person
Skills and experience	Using the phone and switchboard Knowledge of the pass system Knowledge of incoming delivery procedure	Ability to construct rotas Selling skills Technical knowledge of equipment and tools Knowledge of ordering process Management skills	Using the phone Targeting customers Selling skills Knowledge of sales process

These descriptions are not very complete, and you can probably add some elements of your own to each job and person description. For some of these, it would be reasonably easy to check if people have the knowledge, experience and skills by examining their experience and qualifications. But there are also some underlying skills and abilities that they will clearly need in order to be successful.

For the service engineer, these skills could be set down in a person specification including general management skills, communication skills, planning skills, mechanical skills, administrative skills and so on.

The planning and mechanical skills are pretty obvious, but which skills do you think contribute most to job success in each case? Well, it might surprise you to learn that in an extensive study of service engineers in a large heavy-lifting equipment company, verbal reasoning (i.e. communication) proved to be the most powerful predictor of job success. The same was also true for the telephone sales staff. Sometimes, the links can be surprising. In a study of applicants for a car components assembly line, verbal reasoning was found to be the most important predictor of success.

So, if you have been asked to sit a verbal reasoning test, then you can be pretty certain that verbal reasoning, at least as a contributory factor towards general ability, has been identified as a key factor in success, probably because of the importance of communication skills in the job.

Summary

- There are two types of psychometric test – aptitude/ability tests and personality tests.
- The 'science' of testing means that not only are tests systematically designed, but test designers need to pay attention to issues of reliability and validity.
- Tests should be administered and scored in a standardised way following strict instructions.
- Verbal reasoning tests are used mainly in selection and recruitment, owing to their ability to predict performance in some jobs. However, as with all forms of psychometric testing, they are also being used in longer-term career development.

In the next chapter, we will review the nature of verbal reasoning, along with the theory of general mental ability and intelligence.

The nature of verbal reasoning

In the last chapter, we reviewed the nature of psychometric tests and how they are used. In this chapter we will examine some of the underlying theory behind the concept of verbal reasoning, before examining the different types of verbal reasoning test. This is important because we need to understand the nature of verbal reasoning and how it relates to performance in the workplace.

To do this, we shall examine:

- The nature of general mental ability
- The three key aspects of general mental ability
- What is meant by verbal reasoning
- The main types of aptitude test
- Key components of verbal reasoning

The nature of general mental ability

It is pretty obvious that mental abilities vary enormously between different people and influence their success in life. Every day, we make judgements about the mental abilities of other people. Throughout your life, other people have made decisions that affect you, based on their assessment of your abilities. The list is probably pretty long and will include parents, teachers, bosses and employers. But how do we measure an individual's mental abilities? In fact, many of our judgements are subjective or are based on their previous academic success, which is why qualifications figure so highly in our thinking.

In the fields of clinical and educational psychology, the

issues are too important to leave to chance. The diagnosis of psychological or educational difficulties early enough to allow effective treatment was one of the driving forces behind the development of psychometric testing. The first person to have taken a more systematic or 'scientific' approach to measuring some aspect of human behaviour or capability was a French psychologist called Binet, who was interested in the differences between children which affected educational performance. The focus of his interest was in the skills, judgement, comprehension and ability to reason which he felt distinguished achievers and non-achievers. He invented the term 'intelligence quotient' (IQ) to describe these characteristics, and he went on in 1905 to develop the first test to measure them objectively. This test was eventually revised to produce the now famous Stanford-Binet IQ test.

The idea that you can measure the intelligence of an individual, using a single test and one measure, was of course very attractive to large organisations, so much so that by the end of the First World War several million people had undergone such tests when seeking to enlist in the Forces. The validity of this approach was further strengthened by the results of studies on twins that suggested that genetic factors contributed at least 50% to an individual's level of intelligence.

In the years following, the relative contribution of environment and upbringing towards intelligence was fiercely debated, not least because of the catastrophic adoption of the concept of the 'genetic basis for intelligence' by the Nazis and later the demonstration of strong cultural bias in intelligence tests. In the UK, this was reflected in the move away from selection tests in the form of the 'Eleven Plus' examination in education towards the philosophy of non-selection and the comprehensive school system. Nowadays, the concept of pure IQ has been somewhat discredited as too simplistic, and most modern psychologists view intelligence as a more complex, composite issue, preferring to use the term *general mental ability.*

The three key aspects of general mental ability

Research in the area of intelligence testing has consistently demonstrated that there are three main aptitude domains: Verbal, Numerical and Abstract Reasoning Ability.

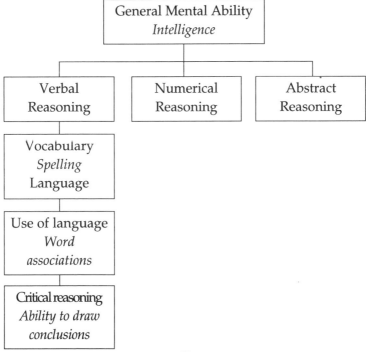

Verbal and Numerical Reasoning assess the ability to use words and numbers in a rational way, correctly identifying logical relationships between words and numbers and drawing conclusions from them.

Abstract Reasoning assesses the ability to identify logical connections between abstract spatial relationships and geometric patterns. Many psychologists argue that Abstract Reasoning tests assess the purest form of 'intelligence', that is to say they are the least affected by educational experience and assess what some might term 'innate' reasoning ability – the ability to solve abstract, logical problems that require no prior knowledge or educational experience.

These three categories are the ones that are focused on in terms of testing in most organisations. They also together comprise a rounded and comprehensive selection of a person's general ability as it relates to work-based skills. This is not to say that in some specific jobs, other abilities may not be required, such as mechanical or spatial ability. However, this trio seems to typify the ones that are required to a greater or lesser degree in most jobs.

What is meant by verbal reasoning?

Let us examine the concept of verbal reasoning more closely. It is your understanding of words and the relationships between words, so it involves all aspects of language such as vocabulary, spelling, and word comprehension association. At the highest level, tests of verbal ability test the ability to reason with words.

What are verbal ability tests used for? Using words is at the basis of so many of our work-related skills. Whether it be spoken or written, most of us have to develop a facility with words in order to make sense of the world and to communicate well. These skills are particularly relevant in jobs therefore that involve a great deal of communication, both written and oral. These include sales and any aspect of customer service, including telesales. For similar reasons, nearly all senior executive posts and all management positions will involve both verbal and written communication as a core set of skills.

The main types of aptitude and ability test

If you think about the range of skills you have developed in your lifetime to date, it is obvious that the talents of the human race cover an incredible and diverse range. We each use a massive repertoire of abilities just to get on with our daily lives. Some of these skills are perceptual (e.g. vision), whereas others are physical (psychomotor) and involve strength, stamina and body control. However, for most of us at work, it is the mental or *cognitive* skills that are by far the most important.

The last fifty years have seen an explosive growth in the development of tests that assess these abilities and there are many thousands of commercial tests available to assess the various aspects of ability and aptitude we discussed above. Because there are so many, it is useful to group them into some main categories.

'Ability tests' is a generic term for all tests of maximum performance (as distinct from habitual performance or personality tests). But within this whole category we can distinguish three main types of test:

- Tests of general or fluid intelligence
- Tests of overall or underlying aptitude
- Attainment tests

Intelligence (IQ) tests

For most of this century it has been assumed that there is some single overarching innate capability that underwrites our ability to learn and master most cognitive skills, referred to as the *intelligence quotient* or IQ. As discussed earlier in this chapter, the whole industry of psychometric testing really began with the notion of intelligence testing.

As mentioned above, the original notion of IQ has now been discredited and psychologists tend to use the notion of 'fluid intelligence' to explain that our ability to learn or master one specific area is related to our ability to master any other.

There are tests that focus on and attempt to measure this fluid intelligence. The line of reasoning is clear. If we know your score on such a test, we can infer your ability to perform a whole range of cognitive tasks. That is then a good basis for predicting other abilities.

Aptitude tests

Another school of thought believes that we should look at more specific aspects of general cognitive ability. As well as giving more detailed information, these specific abilities are more closely work related, and from them we can predict more accurately a person's likely performance in work tasks.

These measure natural ability or the potential to learn a skill or a set of skills. They focus on our underlying ability, but applied to specific areas. They should not require specialist knowledge or learning. Some of the typical things that get measured include the three areas of *Numerical, Verbal* and *Abstract reasoning* identified earlier, but also:

Critical reasoning the ability to draw inferences from data of various kinds

Accuracy – the ability to check or classify information. Checking the accuracy of police reports or computer programmes would be examples.

Other, more specialised types of test include:

- Mechanical reasoning
- Spatial reasoning
- Hand–eye co-ordination

Modern research has clearly shown that accurate assessment of reasoning ability requires tests to be specifically designed to measure that ability in the population concerned. In other words, we need to be sure that a test has been developed for a specific target group and that the skills being assessed are appropriate. This has some important practical implications for the designers of aptitude tests. Firstly, the test must be developed in the country and culture in which it is intended to be used, to ensure that the items in the test are drawn from a common, shared cultural experience. This gives each candidate an equal opportunity to understand the logic which underlies each item.

Secondly, the test must be designed to match the particular ability range of likely test-takers. A test designed for those of average ability, for example, will not accurately discriminate between people of high ability. For this reason, many aptitude tests are available in different forms to match different levels of ability.

Thirdly, in order to separate out natural aptitude from specific knowledge or experience, a lot of care has to go into the design of tests to ensure that a minimal educational level is needed in order to be able to solve each item correctly. Finally, most types of reasoning test, including verbal reasoning, use a variety of items to ensure the test measures all aspects of reasoning ability, rather than measuring a very specific aptitude such as vocabulary.

Attainment tests

Attainment tests are quite distinct from aptitude tests. They measure skills and knowledge that have already been learned or acquired, and the ability to put that knowledge to use. Attainment can be regarded as the outcome of aptitude or potential applied to particular topics and situations. Attainment tests often test quite specific tasks and abilities, and they can be highly work related.

Examples might include:

- Spelling tests
- Grammar and punctuation tests
- The new written test for learner drivers
- Typing tests

We should also mention that some of the tests that are apparently tests of aptitude could also involve a substantial learned element. This means that strictly speaking, they are also tests of attainment. Tests of mechanical ability fall into this category where aptitude and attainment overlap.

Test batteries

There is one special type of test we should mention. It should be clear now, from what has been discussed above, that to assess any aspect of reasoning we need tests that cover a wide range of abilities. For general mental ability, publishers often provide a collection of tests that measure numerical, verbal and abstract reasoning to provide a more rounded picture of the skills they are looking for. Such a collection is known as a battery of tests or *test battery*.

To provide an insight into the construction of a typical test battery, here are the main groups of items that have been included within a widely available test, administered using computers. The test battery assesses the following elements:

Numerical reasoning – a measure of numerical ability which has been isolated as a component of general reasoning.

Verbal reasoning – a standard verbal reasoning test, which evaluates reasoning and the level of literacy of a candidate.

Filing – this test assesses the ability to file quickly and accurately, through an alphabetical or a numerical test of filing.

Spelling – a standard test offering a choice of different spellings for common English words.

Clerical checking – this test assesses the ability to check words and numbers for accuracy.

Typing test – an on-screen test of typing speed and accuracy.

Key components of verbal reasoning
How is verbal reasoning tested? In fact this type of test comes in a number of different forms, which are usually combined. They can be:

- **Spelling, grammar, vocabulary**. As such they are nearer to attainment tests, rather than tests of aptitude. They can also include tests of accuracy. These are justified where the skills tested are a necessary component of the job in question. Data entry would be an example. Secretarial jobs requiring people to write letters or other forms of written communication are also relevant.
- **Comprehension/relationships between words.** These are the most common types of test to look at verbal aptitude, and can be used for a whole range of jobs that involve verbal (or written) communication.
- **Verbal critical reasoning**. This is the 'highest' level, which looks at reasoning and logical argument. These types of test are relevant where people have to deal with large amounts of complex data and argument, and particularly where they have to draw inferences or conclusions from them.

Summary

In this chapter we have examined the concept of general mental ability or intelligence and some of the historical background to intelligence testing. We have identified the fact that general mental ability is now generally split into three main categories: verbal, numerical and abstract reasoning. Tests of aptitude and ability can be split into three main categories:

- Tests of general or fluid intelligence
- Tests of overall or underlying aptitude
- Attainment tests

The main components of verbal reasoning tests fall into the following headings:

- Spelling, grammar, vocabulary.
- Comprehension/relationships between words.
- Verbal critical reasoning.

In the next chapter, we will go on to describe in more detail the features and characteristics of verbal reasoning tests.

Verbal reasoning tests

In the last chapter, we explored the underlying nature of verbal reasoning and its relationship to general mental ability. As we mentioned at the beginning of this book, amongst the two most important questions that people ask about tests of aptitude are:

- What do they look like?
- How do I measure up?

We will look at the first of these two questions in this chapter, and at the second one in the next chapter. In this chapter we will examine some of the main components of verbal reasoning tests and some of the main tests used by organisations to test verbal reasoning abilities.

The typical types of question found in verbal reasoning tests

A major factor in overcoming anxiety for many people is knowing what to expect. To help with this, we shall look at the typical types of question (or item, as they are called) that appear in tests.

In tests of attainment the questions take a fairly predictable form, depending on the type of attainment in question.

Spelling items
Among the most common are questions on spelling:

Example

Choose the correct spelling:

a. accommodate   b. accommadate   c. acomadate
d. acommadate

Answer: A

? Test Yourself

Choose the correct spelling for each:

1. a. desiese   b. disease   c. desease   d. disiese
2. a. eligible   b. elligible   c. eligable   d. elagable
3. a. shedule   b shedyule   c. schedule   d. schedool
4. a. rhythm   b. rithem   c. rhitham   d. rhythmn
5. a. questionnaire   b. questionairre   c. questionaire
    d. questionnairre

Missing words items

Here, test takers are provided with a sentence in which one
or two gaps have been left. The task is simply to decide
what the missing word or words are. These items may in
fact test a variety of different things such as spelling,
grammar and word association.

Example

The students received _____ _____

A	B	C	D
there	their	their	there
awords	awards	awords	awards

Answer: B

? Test Yourself

Choose the correct word to complete these sentences:

6. He . . . to complete the report by Tuesday.
   a. As   b. has   c. must   d. None of these
7. They did not bring . . . money with them.
   a they're   b their   c there   d None of these

Alphabetical order items

These items are often used in clerical tests to measure accuracy under strict time conditions.

Example

Put the letters of VAUXHALL in alphabetical order

Answer: AAHLLUV

? Test Yourself

8. Put the letters of the word MISTAKE in alphabetical order . . .

   Put these words in alphabetical order :
9. a. MORANT   b. MORRIS   c. MORGAN
   d. MORONEY   e. MOULTON
   a.PRAJAPATI   b.POWROZNYK   c.PRAXMARER
   d.PREMJI   e.POZYLO
10. a. PRAJAPATI   b. POWROZNYK   c. PRAXMARER
    d. PREMJI   e. POZYLO

Meaning of words (synonyms, opposites)

These questions will assess your overall vocabulary and usually simply ask you identify words with a similar or opposite meaning.

Example

Enormous means (the same as)
a. Small b. huge c. normal d. enlarged

Answer: B

? Test Yourself

Which word means the same as:

11. CLOSE
    a. imminent b. far c. near d. distant
12. FIX
    a. sort b. put c. add d. mend
13. MOIST
    a. wet b. damp c. soaking d. water

Which word means the opposite of:

14. BORROW
    a. give b. loan c. receive d. lend
15. LOSE
    a. discover b. find c. retrieve d. mislay

Word associations

This type of question features in many verbal reasoning tests.

Examples

Water is to glass as clothes are to ...
a. Shop b. wool c. hangar d. wardrobe

Answer: D, because a glass *contains* water, so a wardrobe *contains* clothes.

Another way this type of question can be presented is to

present two words on one line, requiring the test-taker to choose two words from a lower line, one from each half, e.g.

VISA   COUNTRY

Passport   ticket   nation   Journey   holiday   concert

Answer: You need a **ticket** to go to a **concert**

? Test Yourself

16. What 3 letters can go before each of these to make a word ? . . .,
    bate claim cure

17. What 3-letter word can go before each of these:
    coat light hot

18. **Here** is to **where** as **now** is to?
    a. when   b. time   c. then   d. never

19. **Phone** is to **ear** as **TV** is to?
    a. picture   b. see   c. eye   d. watch

20. **Book** is to **read** as **microwave** is to?
    a. kitchen   b. meal   c. electric   d. cook

Odd one out

Used to test your ability to identify connections between words and to reason, they do not usually require an explanation. Do not be tempted to guess.

Example

Which is the odd one out?
a. box   b. paper   c. jug   d. envelope   e. bag

Answer: C, all the rest are made of paper

? ## Test Yourself

Which is the odd one out?

21. a. candle b. coal c. wood d. heat

22. a. say b. obey o. instruct d. order

23. a. read b. book c. paper d. novel

24. a. Jersey b. Belgium c. Cyprus d. Australia

25. a. dog b. cat c. shark d. tiger

Mixed sentence or word swap items

In this type of test, you will be presented with a series of sentences in which the positions of two words have been altered so that the sentence no longer makes sense. Your task is to read the sentence carefully and underline the two words that should be swapped.

Example

Too much water ruins growth, if it is also poor but there is a drought.

Answer: Too much water ruins plant growth, **if** it is also poor **but** there is a drought. It should read 'Too much water ruins plant growth, **but** it is also poor **if** there is a drought.'

? ## Test Yourself

26. Professional control offers an important benefit: the freedom to choose clients and collect fees, without state practice.

27. The company wants to develop specialist subscription professions for the financial business community and programmes such as doctors.

28. Amidst last-minute fears that the riots would spread, growing peace talks were held with the organisation's representatives last night.

Hidden sentences

These items each consist of a single sentence, to which has been added a number of irrelevant words. These words are scattered throughout the sentence to hide the original sentence. Your task is to underline the words that form the original sentence, or to identify the first and the last two or three words. Usually a number is given in brackets to indicate the length of the required sentence.

Example

See replacing doors towards is not west something happening you can buy hear easily afford everything tomorrow (9)

Answer: See **replacing doors** towards **is** not west **something** happening **you can** buy hear **easily afford** everything **tomorrow**

? Test Yourself

29. My if he watch sport stopped its just at the day we walked same time ten past ten as the town hall tomorrow clock (12)

30. At one end the of the talk I found out why it difficult to understand concentration and some so lost gave interest sharing together (10)

31. When traditionally Scotland the English are castles museum have bought one more newspapers per capita of population growth towards than anywhere else wherever else other she is in Europeans (12)

Sentence sequence items

In this form of test, you are provided with a piece of text, consisting of three to four sentences or phrases, whose order has been altered, so that the text is out of sequence. Your task is to read the complete text and work out the correct sequence. These questions are normally strictly time-limited, effectively measuring how quickly you can scan the sentences and make sense of them.

Example

(1) To thicken the sauce, put an extra heaped teaspoon into the dissolved mixture. (2) Pour quarter of a pint of water onto the granules, stirring all the time. (3) Keep stirring until all the granules are dissolved. (4) Put two heaped teaspoons of the granules into a measuring jug.

Answer: 4, 2, 3, 1

? **Test Yourself**

32. (1) The very name is strictly controlled. (2) The term used to describe the way it is made – the méthode champenoise – can only be applied to wine from there. (3) Champagne is in a class of its own. (4) It can only be given to wine from the Champagne region in France.

33. (1) And with a CD-player fitted as standard, you don't need to be quiet about it either. (2) It's chic, practical and the most fuel efficient in its class. (3) If freedom is what you're looking for, you're looking at the right car. (4) If you'd like to know more, phone this number now.

34. (1) Confidential records will be then be kept, but only using a number which staff will allocate to users of the service. (2) Yes, totally. (3) At first, verbal contact will be made between the client and a staff member. (4) Is the service confidential?

Critical reasoning

Critical reasoning is the ability to use logical argument. It tests whether you are able to draw inferences and conclusions from arguments and data. Verbal critical reasoning tests are often based around passages of text or sentences, and questions are then asked about them.

Example

'We need to save time getting there so we'd better go by plane.'

Is the assumption that follows taken for granted (yes/no)?

'Travel by plane is more convenient than travel by train.'

Answer: NO. This assumption is not made in the statement as the statement is about saving time and has nothing to do with convenience. (Source: Watson Glaser)

? **Test Yourself**

'All Venusians are tall. Some Venusians are not friendly.'

Decide whether each statement is:
a. definitely true   b. definitely false   c. can't tell

35. Friendly Venusians are tall.

36. No Venusians are tall and friendly

'The white paper is full of promises to regulate rogue traders. Regulation however – even if it does happen – will not solve the problem of poor services. Only the power of the consumer can do that.'

For each statement, decide if it is:

   a. definitely true b. probably true c. can't tell d. probably
   false e. definitely false

37. The government will regulate poor services

38. Consumer power can solve the problem

00. Regulation is a good thing

Answers to the practice examples

1	b	26	control,
2	a		practice
3	c	27	professions,
4	a		programmes
5	a	28	last-minute,
6	b		growing
7	b	29	My watch
8	AEIKMST		stopped ...
9	acdbe		town hall
10	beacd		clock
11	c	30	I found it ...
12	d		so lost
13	b		interest
14	d	31	Traditionally
15	b		the English ...
16	pro		than other
17	red		Europeans
18	a	32	3 1 4 2
19	c	33	3 2 1 4
20	d	34	4 2 3 1
21	d	35	a
22	b	36	b
23	a	37	c
24	b	38	a
25	c	39	b

From these practice questions, you should already be beginning to get used to the sort of questions you will encounter in the real thing. You may also be starting to get some idea of which categories of item you find harder to do. If they seem too simple, remember that at this stage, we have not included one essential ingredient of verbal reasoning tests – a limit on the time available. With limited time, it becomes harder to make instant decisions and mistakes are more likely.

Commonly used tests

In this section, we shall provide a brief resume of a range of tests commonly used in employment practice. The purpose of this is to give you an idea, in broad terms, of what you might expect. It should also help to understand some of the common features and the differences between such tests. For each of these tests, information is provided under the following headings:

- General details
- Uses
- Format
- What does it measure?

The sections below are basic descriptions and should not be taken for professional evaluations of the tests or test batteries. If you would like to see such a thing, the British Psychological Society (address in the appendix) does provide objective evaluations for professional users.

In fact, it is not unusual these days for test publishers to provide test-takers with practice papers. This is precisely because they want you to know what you are being asked to do, but also because they want to preserve the fairness and objectivity of the actual tests.

General intelligence tests

As we have emphasised elsewhere, these are used less and less these days, having been replaced, on the whole, by more specific and specialised tests. However, the most famous and well used of those available is:

The Stanford-Binet Intelligence Scale (4th edition)

General details
Produced in 1986, the industry standard IQ test produced by Riverside Publishing has been greatly modified since its creation.

Uses
It assesses intelligence and cognitive abilities, but provides a single instrument that can be used with all age groups.

Format
The time taken depends on the number of sub-tests (15 tests, spanning 4 areas) taken. The four areas are Verbal, Quantitative and Abstract Reasoning, along with Short-term Memory.

What does it measure?
This edition is the most extensive revision of the Binet-Simon IQ Scale since its inception. Major changes include the elimination of the age scale, incorporation of four area scores as well as a composite score, and the incorporation of recent advances in psychometric theory within the design.

Basic tests of aptitude and ability

Employment Aptitude Survey (EAS)

General details
Produced by the Test Agency, this series of tests covers a very wide range of abilities, not all of which will be useful or needed in many real applications.

Uses
Suitable for all levels, including secretarial, clerical, retail and technical sales staff. The tests provide 'a battery of aptitude measures designed for the selection of applicants at all levels ... is also ideal for apprenticeship selection and general guidance.'

Format
Ten 5-minute tests.

What does it measure?
A range of aptitudes:
- Verbal comprehension
- Numerical ability
- Visual pursuit
- Visual speed and accuracy
- Spatial visualisation

- Numerical reasoning
- Verbal reasoning
- Word fluency
- Manual speed and accuracy
- Symbolic reasoning

The GMAT® Computer-Adaptive Test (CAT)

General details
If you are or have been a student on a business studies or management course, you may have sat a verbal reasoning test as part of the GMAT or Graduate Management Admission Test. Strictly speaking it is more of an attainment test, but it does contain comprehension and critical reasoning items.

Uses
The GMAT is specially designed to help graduate business schools assess the qualifications of those who seek admission to study for an MBA or into another advanced business/management programme, and used in some way by more than 1,500 graduate management programmes around the world.

Format
The test is administered in a computer-based form at special testing locations throughout the world. The test can take as long as four hours to complete. The questions are divided into the following sections:

Verbal
  Sentence correction
  Reading comprehension
  Critical reasoning

Quantitative
  Problem solving
  Data sufficiency

Analytical writing
  Analysis of an issue
  Analysis of an argument

What does it measure?
The GMAT report contains four score for verbal, quantitative, total, and analytical writing. Verbal and quantitative scores are reported on scales ranging from 0 to 60 and the total score is reported on a scale ranging from 200 to 800.

General Reasoning Test (GRT2)

General details

Issued by Psytech International, this test offers 'a comprehensive, detailed and accurate measure of mental ability ... designed to assess reasoning power for those of general ability'.

Uses

Suitable for a general education level, covering a wide range of abilities and applications. Focused on mental ability rather than any specific attainments, the test assesses the minimum level needed for many jobs.

Format

Two tests of ten minutes and one of eight minutes.

What does it measure?

Verbal, numerical and abstract reasoning

Test batteries for graduate and managerial posts

We should make the point that many of the general tests above can be appropriate for graduate and managerial level positions. However, there are some test batteries that focus particularly on this group. Here are some typical ones.

Graduate Reasoning Test (GRT1)

General details

Published by Psytech International and designed to assess people of graduate ability, it only needs a general level of ability to complete, so it can be used to identify people of potential for development or progression.

Uses
The test has been designed to 'assess high level reasoning ability' at graduate and managerial level.

Format
Two tests of ten minutes and one of eight minutes.

What does it measure?
Verbal, numerical and abstract reasoning

Advance Managerial Tests (AMT)

General details
Published by Saville and Holdsworth, these tests are designed to 'assess ... across a range of functions', such as the understanding of the meaning of words, interpretation of complex verbal information, interpretation of complex numerical data and numerical reasoning.

Uses
Designed for managers, professional and graduates.

Format
A series of tests ranging from 20 minutes to 35 minutes. Calculators are allowed, which emphasises

that it is the reasoning rather than the operational or computational skill which is being tested.

What does it measure?
Verbal application
Verbal analysis
Numerical reasoning
Numerical analysis

Critical Reasoning Test Battery (CRTB)

General details
Produced by Psytech International, these tests provide 'a detailed and accurate measure of critical reasoning ... they can be used to assess general ability and to identify particular areas of strength and weakness.'

Uses
Used to identify management potential, for graduate recruitment, and senior management assessment.

Format
Two tests, of 20 minutes and 30 minutes.

What does it measure?
Verbal critical reasoning and numerical critical reasoning.

Watson Glaser Critical thinking appraisal

General details
Produced by the Test Agency, Oxford Psychologist Press, this battery measures five aspects of the ability to think critically.

Uses
Applicable across a wide range of higher level jobs at graduate and management level.

Format
80 items in 5 sections. Can be timed or untimed, taking 40 minutes if timed.

What does it measure?
Drawing inferences from facts
Recognising assumptions
Reasoning by deduction
Reasoning by interpretation
Discriminating strong and weak arguments

Other forms of assessment

We have focussed mostly on those aspects of aptitude and ability that can be tested by psychometric tests. Yet they are not the only method used to test ability.

Work sample tests – these are tests designed around performance of real but representative job tasks. They tend to be used for relatively simple jobs where the individual tasks can be easily identified and specified. They are useful because of their obvious relevance, but they can be expensive and time consuming. They also need experienced and trained people to administer them.

Assessment centres – these are events organised around a range of activities that are designed to provide quality information about all relevant aspects of the participants' abilities and skills. They may include the use of standard psychometric tests, but they also generate data about underlying abilities via observed behaviour in individual and group activities, case studies, etc. They are used for external recruitment and for internal promotion and development. Their advantage is that they can be designed to elicit the relevant information very accurately, and based on real behaviour. The disadvantage is that they are expensive and time consuming.

Competence-based interviews – these are structured interviews, designed to elicit your knowledge, skills and effectiveness in relation to defined job competencies. This is done by focusing on your experience, approach and achievements in real working contexts.

360 degree appraisal – this is a means of collecting information about your performance from key stakeholders. This can include subordinates, line managers, colleagues, and customers. To obtain this kind of quality information requires substantial resources, including time and expertise to administer. Also, it doesn't replace information about underlying aptitude and ability, as it focuses on how this manifests in behaviour in the real working environment.

As you can see from the above, many of these techniques are aimed at providing high quality information, and most of them deliver that promise. However, by themselves they don't provide information that replaces objective psychometric data, but instead offer information that supplements it. This is why many of these techniques are used in conjunction with tests of aptitude and ability, not to replace them.

Summary

In this chapter, we have described some of the key questions that feature in most verbal reasoning tests. The main items you are likely to encounter include:

- Spelling items
- Missing words items
- Alphabetical order items
- Meaning of words (synonyms, opposites) items
- Word association items
- Odd one out items
- Mixed sentence or word swap Items
- Hidden sentences
- Sentence sequence items
- Critical reasoning items

We have also described some of the more common and typical commercial tests that you might face, along with some other methods of assessing aptitude and ability. In the next chapter, we will review the test experience itself and provide advice on how to get the best out of it.

Preparing for tests

In the last chapter we examined some of the key verbal reasoning tests and test batteries to give you an insight into their format and their main uses. In this chapter, we will examine the test experience itself to prepare you for the event.

There is no doubt that sitting tests can be stressful for many people. The reasons can be varied – fear of the unknown, a hate of formal 'test' situations left over from schooldays, personal insecurity – but whatever the cause, if you do feel nervous just remember that this is a perfectly natural reaction. More to the point, just like stage fright, you can deal with your anxiety by being prepared. We shall deal with this possibility by explaining the procedures for test administration, the simple steps you can take to prepare yourself, your rights as a test-taker and finally how you can get the most out of the experience.

Test administration

Aptitude tests are generally used as part of the selection process for jobs or as part of an internal development process. In either case, it is common for employers to use a battery of tests (i.e. more than one). Usually this involves several aptitude tests followed by a personality questionnaire.

The process you will go through when asked to take an aptitude test is pretty standard, because organisations need to take special care to make sure everyone goes through the same experience. This is why to some the whole experience can be rather formal and off-putting, just like an examination. This is probably what you will experience:

1. A qualified test administrator will introduce you to the test. They will usually explain the reason for the test, even if you have been provided with the information previously.
2. They will then check that you have everything you need for the test, such as the test itself, an answer sheet or book, pencils and/or pens, erasers, paper for scribbling on.
3. You will then be asked to record your name and date on the answer sheet, perhaps with some biographical details.
4. The administrator will then read out the instructions at the beginning of the questionnaire. Follow these carefully, even if you think they look simple. These typically include (a) how to record your answers and change them and (b) some advice on the need to avoid guessing and to not spend too long on questions. Once they have read through the instructions, they will ask if you have any questions.
5. You will then be asked to begin. During the test, the administrator will walk round the room to check that you are completing the answer sheet correctly. They are not checking to see if you are 'cheating'.
6. When the test has been completed, the administrator will take in all the materials, thank you for sitting the test and perhaps remind you what is going to happen to them.

All this is pretty simple. One key difference between aptitude or ability tests and personality questionnaires is that the former are usually timed, whereas personality questionnaires are open, so you can take as long as you like. A short questionnaire can take as little as 10 minutes, whereas the longer ones can take up to 45 minutes.

Preparing for tests

So, you have been short-listed for that important job and asked to take an aptitude or verbal reasoning test, perhaps together with some other assessments. You may feel a little nervous. Remember, this is perfectly normal and easily treated. There is a lot you can do to prepare for the test itself, e.g.

- Get clued up about the job and the test(s)
- Relax and be yourself

Getting clued up about the job and the tests
Organisations don't use aptitude tests just for the sake of it. They use these tests because the skills being assessed have been linked directly to job success. However, they are not the only thing used to assess suitability.

As we have already mentioned, it is quite normal for test publishers to provide practice and familiarisation material. Don't be afraid to ask for this if it is not provided automatically. Failing that, you are entitled to ask about the nature of the test – what kinds of test; what do they consist of; are there any descriptions or guidelines, and so on. Use what practice material is available (or the nearest you can find). This has two benefits. The first is to help your brain get used to thinking in the right kind of ways required for the test. The second is really about reassurance. Again, once you know what to expect, and you have 'had a go', it means that there are no unpleasant surprises, and this helps you to do your best.

Relaxing and being yourself

Acting naturally and getting yourself into a fairly relaxed frame of mind is probably the best advice anyone can give to help you 'do well'. One important way in which you can develop yourself in relation to aptitude and ability testing is to make sure that you perform to the best of your ability in a real testing situation. For many people, ignorance of the process and anxiety during the testing mean that they do not perform to their full potential.

Before the test, to get yourself into the best frame of mind possible, you should:

- **Find out about the arrangements.** First check the obvious and basic details like the start time and the location. Also ask about the duration of the test(s) themselves. Check if there are any special considerations, or if you need to bring any equipment, such as calculators. You shouldn't need to, but checking these details is always reassuring.
- **Get a good night's rest** and avoid anything that may upset your normal mental balance, such as pub crawls. Do something relaxing the day or night before, as this always helps. Different people achieve this in different ways such as exercise, leisure or other means of relaxation.
- **Arrive with plenty of time to spare**, but not so much that you have hours to worry about the test(s).
- **If anxiety is getting the better of you**, make a

conscious effort to breathe slowly and deeply and to turn your attention to something else if possible. Use every opportunity to give yourself positive messages. There is no doubt that if you tell yourself that you will make a mess of it, you are more than half way to doing just that! Many people have supportive friends or loved ones who can help in this.

During the test itself, here are some golden rules that you should follow:

- **Make sure you know what to do**. Listen to the instructions closely and read the instructions carefully before the test starts. Do not skim read at this stage – you can overlook important details and make silly mistakes. Some people find it helpful to underline key words in the instructions. If in doubt, ask the test administrator.
- **Don't assume anything**. Even if you have taken the test before, please don't assume the instructions are the same. The test may have changed or it may be in a different form.
- **Work quickly and in a focused way**. Once the test begins, work as quickly and accurately as you can. Check and double-check that you are filling in the correct boxes in the answer grid. If you are uncertain, enter your best reasoned choice.
- **Don't get hung up on particular questions**. If you find some questions very difficult, move on quickly and come back to them later. Avoid the temptation

to keep working away at a question that is frustrating you.

- **Concentrate.** Keep working as hard as you can throughout the test. Concentrate on the test and nothing else. Don't allow yourself to be distracted. If you have any spare time when you have finished, go back and check all your answers.
- **Be positive.** Don't allow anxiety or worry over the results of previous tests or examinations to affect your performance. Think yourself into the frame of mind you experience at the end of a good day's work, and don't allow yourself to be beaten before you begin.

After the test, you should:

- **Stop worrying.** It never did you any good in the past. Remember that employers don't just select people on the basis of high test scores. Get on with the rest of the selection process.
- **Try to learn from the experience**. If appropriate try to get some feedback.

Know your rights

No organisation can force you to take tests. They are obliged to secure your agreement to take any test and because the results are of an extremely personal nature, they have a legal and ethical responsibility to make sure the results are used, interpreted, stored and disposed of safely.

You can of course refuse to complete tests, but in reality the organisation will be within its rights to reject your application. Nevertheless you do have well-defined rights as a test-taker. Here are a few guidelines about the correct use of tests.

Information Responsible organisations should take special steps to ensure there are no misunderstandings and that the test-takers fully understand the purpose of the tests. They have a duty to make sure you are fully informed about the nature of the tests, their role in the process and likely duration, the arrangements for taking the tests and what will be done with the results. If in doubt, ask!

Test administration The facilities used for the administration of any test are important. You have a right to be provided with a quiet, well-lit and ventilated room, complete with comfortable and well-spaced tables and chairs. The test itself must be carried out by a qualified administrator and free from any interruptions, otherwise the test itself is really invalidated.

Equal opportunities The issue of the cultural or sexual sensitivity of tests is a difficult one. In law it is the responsibility of the organisation to check that the tests used are not discriminatory because they contain elements that are culturally biased (typically questions that ask you about your favourite activities). If you have any concerns, you do have a right to check that the test has been screened for cultural bias by testing it amongst different groups.

However in some situations, different cultural types may show personality differences that can be linked to job performance. Here, the organisation may be quite justified in using such tests, but would need to be very confident about their validity, measured in terms of job performance and success.

If in doubt, you could seek guidance from an expert in the field or from the Equal Opportunities Commission.

Special needs   If you have any special needs, discuss these with the organisation. You do not need to suffer in silence and you may be pleasantly surprised by the alternatives that are available. For example, computerised versions with large text for the visually impaired can make life a lot easier. If you suffer from dyslexia, they may be able to provide someone who will read through the text.

Test feedback   Ideally all test-takers should be given an opportunity to receive feedback and to discuss the results of the test. In reality, where these tests are used for selection, there may be too many candidates or the organisation may not wish to reveal too much about the selection criteria used.

Even if you do not receive formal feedback, you may receive it informally during the interview through any questions that relate to the type of tasks you are good at. Watch for these and remember this is where your preparation can really pay off.

Finally, all candidates should receive the same treatment. This means that restricting detailed feedback to internal candidates because of the numbers involved is very bad selection practice indeed.

Security and access

Your test results are an extremely personal and sensitive form of information. For this reason, the organisation has a duty to ensure that access to the results is restricted only to those people who are qualified to interpret them and those who will actually use the results. In agreeing to take the test, you have only agreed to it being used in the situation that has been requested. The organisation is not at liberty to use the results elsewhere.

The test results should be kept in a secure location, under lock and key, and are from October 1998 subject to the full protection of the Data Protection Act.

Disposal of results

Test results have a limited lifespan. They should not be kept any longer than the event they were required for. You are quite within your rights to ask how long the results will be kept and how they will be disposed of.

Getting the most out of the experience

Whatever the outcome of a process involving the use of psychometric tests, you should take steps to maximise your learning. Even if you fail to get that brilliant job, you should follow up the interview by asking for feedback. Good organisations will normally be open to requests for more information than the simple acceptance or rejection letter. If you are given an opportunity to discuss your performance in detail, make sure you identify the critical factors involved.

- Ask about the relative importance of the test results compared to experience and specific skills.
- Identify the key qualities they were looking for.
- Focus sharply on the issues involved with these critical factors. Don't just get annoyed – ask them directly what they were looking for and how this compared with their assessment of you.
- Listen to their advice on how to improve your personal profile.

Even if you don't receive this sort of feedback, try to be objective about your performance using the same framework. You may find it helpful to involve a trusted colleague or boss in this process. Above all, be determined to learn more about yourself from the experience and identify clear action points for the future. Even if you don't get the job, gaining more insight into your most marketable qualities and those which perhaps work against you in some situations will equip you better for the next application. Successful managers often have profiles that change over time. One secret to their success is almost certainly that they do pay attention to the way others see them, that they recognise barriers to progress and are able to identify development opportunities for the future.

Summary

In this chapter we have examined the main factors involved in taking tests and how to ensure you get the best out of them, i.e.

- How tests are administered
- How to prepare effectively for the tests
- Your rights as a test-taker
- After the test, how to get the most out of tests

In the next chapter we shall provide you with a sample verbal reasoning test to familiarise you with the type of questions you will typically encounter in these tests. It will also provide you with more insight into how tests are constructed. Perhaps more importantly, the results will link with the final chapter, in which we will show you how to gain more control over your personal abilities and their relationship to career preferences.

Test yourself

In the last chapter, we reviewed the test experience itself to give you an idea of what to expect and to provide some insight into the way aptitude tests are used. We stressed the fact that anxiety over taking 'tests' was quite natural, but something that everyone can deal with.

One of the best ways of dealing with someone's fear of the unknown is to take them through the process concerned and explain what is involved in order to de-mystify it. This is what we propose to do in this chapter by taking you through a sample verbal reasoning test. The results you gain from doing this should also be useful for the last chapter.

Before you begin

You have now read about aptitude and ability – what it is and what it comprises. If we focus mainly on cognitive (mental) abilities, we should think about the following.

Compared to the rest of the population, how would you rate yourself in the following areas?

	above average	average	below average
Verbal reasoning			
Spelling & Vocabulary			
Word associations			
Critical reasoning			
Numerical reasoning			
Abstract reasoning			

Let us now see if your own assessment matches the results of a trial verbal reasoning test.

A Simple Verbal Reasoning Test (SVRT)

The following questionnaire has been designed to provide a rough guide to your verbal reasoning skills in a number of key areas. It has however been deliberately simplified and the results should not be taken as a definitive evaluation of your verbal reasoning skills. Please read the instructions carefully before embarking on the test.

? ## Test Yourself
Instructions
This is a self-administered questionnaire concerning your verbal reasoning skills. It consists of 72 questions divided into three sections. Each question has a limited choice (3-5) of possible answers.

Please read all the instructions carefully before beginning. Answer each section exactly as described in the questionnaire. For each question, mark the correct box next to the question in pencil.

When answering questions, please remember the following:

- Don't spend too much time deliberating over the questions.
- If you want to change an answer, erase your original response and add your altered response

You have 15 minutes to complete the test. At the end of this time, you should stop and proceed to the section on scoring the test.

Now please begin.

The Test

Section A: Spelling and Vocabulary

A1

Identify and circle the correct spelling for each of the following.

1. a. Rithm   b. rhythm   c. rythm   d. rythmn

2. a. knowledgable   b. knowledgeable   c. nowledgeable   d. knowledgabel

3. a. complementary   b. complimentry   c. complimentery   d. complamentary

4. a. descision   b. decision   c. desision   d. deciscion

5. a. prefference   b. preferance   c. preference   d. preferrence

6. a. arrdvark   b. ardvark   c. ardvaark   d. aardvark

7. a. abcess   b. abses   c. abscess   d. abcesse

8. a. filanthropic   b. filanfropic   c. thilanthropic   d. philanthropic

9. a. effeminate   b. efeminate   c. effemenate   d. effeminnate

10. a. Soroastrianism   b. Zorastrianism   c. Zoroastrianism   d. Zoroastranism

A2

Which of the following words means the same or almost the same as

11. Erudite

a. persuasive   b. confident   c. knowledgeable
d. cantankerous   e. hostile

12. Mercenary
    a. missionary   b. callous   c. adventurous   d. caring
    e. magnanimous

13. Arcane
    a. obtuse   b. obscure   c. circular   d. grandiose
    e. mysterious

14. Fecund
    a. barren   b. fertile   c. filthy   d. meaningful
    e. bright

15. Fatuous
    a. overweight   b. pretentious   c. virulent   d. inane
    e. convincing

16. Audacious
    a. frightening   b. daring   c. horrible   d. awesome
    e. cynical

17. Libertine
    a. personable   b. free-thinking   c. dissolute
    d. debauched   e. democratic

18. Fallacious
    a. necessary   b. theoretical   c. treacherous
    d. erratic   e. erroneous

19. Trepidation
    a. dampness   b. fearlessness   c. fearfulness
    d. maliciousness   e. conscientiousness

20. Phlegmatic
    a. unemotional   b. anxious   c. inflamed
    d. hypothetical   e. inebriated

Section B: Word Associations
B1

Which is the odd one out?

1. a. door   b. kitchen   c. painted   d. garage   e. porch

2. a. sculptor   b. painter   c. singer   d. author
   e. composer

3. a. car   b. train   c. bus   d. plane   e. tram   f. road

4. a. hear   b. taste   c. see   d. food   e. smell

5. a. trousers   b. shirt   c. socks   d. jacket   e. necklace

6. a. elevate   b. lift   c. expand   d. raise   e. promote

7. a. iron   b. copper   c. brass   d. aluminium   e. granite

8. a. fibula   b. tibia   c. radius   d. femur   e. patella

9. a. petulant   b. churlish   c. choleric   d. reticent
   e. truculent

10. a. progress   b. advance   c. develop   d. consolidate
    e. grow

11. a. test   b. examine   c. analyse   d. investigate
    e. probe

12. a. empathic   b. supportive   c. caring   d. understanding
    e. sympathetic

13. a. tenor   b. oregano   c. contralto   d. soprano.
    e. alto

14. a. goal   b. penalty   c. run   d. point   e. try

15. a. spade   b. rake   c. hammer   d. spoon   e. fork

B2

Identify the word which completes the following sentences:

16. Cat is to kitten as dog is to:
    a. Beast   b. bark   c. puppy   d. chase

17. Prisoner is to goal as water is to:
    a. prison   b. drink   c. tap   d. bucket

18. Tall is to height as heavy is to:
    a. scales   b. weight   c. size   d. mass

19. Before is to behind as future is to:
    a. forward   b. advanced   c. ahead   d. imminent

20. Word is to sentence as paragraph is to:
    a. word   b. book   c. chapter   d. tome

21. Over is to under as above is to:
    a. below   b. underneath   c. beneath   d. under

22. Milk is to jug as sugar is to:
    a. spoon   b. bowl   c. cube   d. packet

23. Cow is to bovine as horse is to:
    a. equine   b. stallion   c. feline   d. canine

24. Loud is to loudest as bad is to:
    a. worse   b. better   c. good   d. worst

25. Wine is to grape as vodka is to:
    a. corn   b. rice   c. potato   d. pear

26. Sun is to hot as rain is to:
    a. damp   b. cold   c. wet   d. soaking

27. Square is to rectangle as circle is to:
    a. globe   b. ball   c. sphere   d. oval

28. Cocoon is to chrysalis as shell is to:

a. nut   b. projectile   c. crustacean   d. explosive

29. Confined space is to claustrophobia as open space is to:
    a. agoraphobia   b. nyctophobia   c. arachnophobia
    d. xenophobia   e. agraphobia

30. Fastidious is to critical as abstemious is to:
    a. excessive   b. moderate   c. minimal   d. mercurial
    e. precise

Which *one* of the following has a similar relationship to the two words in brackets

31. **(Second Time)** a. ounce   b. return   c. minute
    d. weight

32. **(Prediction Future)** a. past   b. absence   c. memory
    d. present

33. **(Composer Opera)** a. music   b. author   c. read
    d. novel

34. **(Square Cube)** a. curve   b. circle   c. round   d. sphere

35. **(Track Door)** a. cart   b. step   c. lane   d. back

36. **(Fair Goal)** a. aim   b. unbiased   c. objective
    d. game   e. ground

37. **(Miserly Average)** a. typical   b. mean   c. frugal
    d. ordinary   e. parsimonious

38. **(Push Journalists)** a. press   b. newspaper
    c. pressure   d. editor

39. **(Code Card)** a. bag   b. letter   c. post   d. mail
    e. symbol

40. **(Book Some)** a. seek   b. hand   c. many   d. page
    e. glasses

Section C: Critical reasoning

You are provided below with two pieces of text. You should read each piece of text and then decide whether each of the statements that follows is true (**a**), cannot be determined (**b**) or is false (**c**).

Case A

Recent research undertaken under the auspices of the Psychology Department at Lansdowne College has examined how effective different assessment procedures are in predicting performance at work. In their study psychologists administered various selection techniques to a sample of 65 managers whose performance had been assessed previously using a validated performance appraisal. Of all the methods used a verbal reasoning test was the best predictor of job performance, followed by a structured interview. Personality measures only showed a small relationship with performance and an analysis of handwriting and birth-sign showed no relationship with performance at all.

	(a)	**(b)**	**(c)**
1 Personality tests are useless as an indicator of likely management performance			
2 Candidates with good interview skills are most likely to get the job.			
3 It is not possible to predict management performance.			

		(a)	(b)	(c)
4	Managers who performed less well on the verbal reasoning test tended to have lower job performance ratings.			
5	Handwriting analysis is a valid form of assessment.			
6	It is possible to use performance appraisals as a measure of management performance.			

Case B

A project team of Felton-McGregor, a pharmaceutical company, needed more money and time to complete its project on a major new product. Marketing needed more comprehensive customer information to be able to refine their sales strategy. The product's research and development team, who had almost finished the design phase, needed more information on the most cost-effective constituent chemicals to use. Time and money was at a premium: both teams' demands could not be met. The product manager decided that the remaining budget would be spent on further researching who would buy the product, which in turn would help in deciding on the best materials to use.

	(a)	(b)	(c)
7 The marketing team base their sales strategy on customer information.			
8 The product manager has complete control over the budget.			
9 A single solution would solve both the product and marketing teams' problems.			
10 Existing sales strategies are not considered to be ideal for the new product.			
11 The proposed research on the customer base would result in a budget overspend.			
12 Without information about the cost-effectiveness of constituent chemicals, R&D cannot complete the design on time.			

Scoring your test results

The first thing you need to do is to score your test. The correct answers can be found at the end of this chapter. Add up your correct responses for each section and enter the number of correct responses into the following table:

SECTION	Category	Possible score	Your score
A	Spelling & vocabulary	20	
B	Word associations	40	
C	Critical reasoning	12	
TOTAL		72	

Interpreting the results

Before we turn to your own test scores, we need to explain how scores are used and interpreted when real, commercial tests are used. Most people, when they take any kind of test, are interested to know what their 'score' is and they often assume that the result will be a single number or score that gives the number of right answers, perhaps expressed as a percentage.

In fact, this is rarely true. Of course, as we have pointed out previously, aptitude and ability tests are based on right and wrong answers, but it is not the number of right answers that is the most important thing. In our early discussion of psychometric tests, we identified the fact that these tests were designed, administered and interpreted in a standardised way. If an individual scores 15 out of a maximum of 20 on the test, what does this actually mean? Not a lot, unless it is compared to the way in which other people respond.

For this reason, raw scores on a test are always converted to a 'standardised score' that compares the individual score with the scores of a known group of people, which might be the general population, graduates, managers or people in a particular organisation

It works like this:

Like most variables that occur in the natural world, measurements for a population are distributed in a characteristic way. For instance, if we measured the heights of a large and representative sample of the population, and put the heights on a frequency diagram, they would look like the diagram below.

The shape of this line occurs so often in nature that we give it an official name. It is called the ***normal distribution***. It is

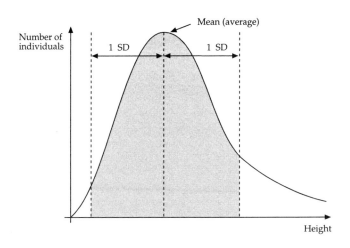

bell-shaped and symmetrical, and the average (or mean) is the highest point on the curve.

Another statistic which is very relevant in this distribution is called the *standard deviation* (SD) and it measures the spread of values in the distribution. It allows us to quantify the number of people in a test who score above or below particular values.

For example, we know that 68% of people will score between plus and minus 1 SD score (the area shown on the diagram). When raw scores are converted to standardised scores, it places the score in relation to the rest of the population. There are two popular ways of doing this:

- *Sten (standard ten) scores*. These 'carve' the distribution up into ten units, with the middle being at 5.5.
- *Percentiles*. These carve the distribution up into 100 units, with the middle being 50.

It is of course vitally important when working with standardised scores to know the group or population used to produce the questionnaire scores. On most test reports you will find a comment that tells you where the *norms* were obtained from. A percentile score on an ability test of 60 (which means scores higher than 60% of the population) is one thing if you are compared with the population as a whole. However, if you are being compared to a graduate population, or a senior management population, then the interpretation will be slightly different.

In many cases, this is not even done by numbers, but by banding, or slicing the distribution into categories (as shown in the diagram above). So quite often, the feedback you get will not be in the form of a number, but might be in the form of a statement like:

- in the top band
- average
- as well as most people ...

Think about the first section of the last chapter where we asked you to evaluate your own aptitude and ability, if you could be reasonably sure you are 'above average', 'average', or 'below average', this is all the information you need.

Rating your scores
So let us see how you did. Set against the general population, the table below will give you an idea of how your results worked out.

SECTION	Category	Below average	Average	Above average
A	Spelling & vocabulary	0–9	10–14	15–20
B	Word associations	0–12	13–28	29–40
C	Critical reasoning	0–2	3–5	6–12
TOTAL		0–23	24–47	48–72

If you think you fall into the graduate or managerial population, expectations would be rather different so you should use the following table as a more useful guide:

SECTION	Category	Below average	Average	Above average
A	Spelling & vocabulary	0–13	14–17	18–20
B	Word associations	0–20	21–32	33–40
C	Critical reasoning	0–3	4–7	8–12
TOTAL		0–36	37–56	57–72

Notice of course that there is less discrimination possible at the higher end of the scale.

When looking at your overall scores, there are a number of things to bear in mind.

1 The scores only make sense if you followed the time guidelines. Time is an important factor. The time you needed gives a measure, not just of the accuracy, but of the fluency with which you can reason with words (in this case). However, it can be useful to know that you are accurate, even if you are slow.

2 These scores have not been standardised rigorously, meaning that we can't compare you to a known population with the accuracy one would expect from a commercial test. So the benchmark information we are providing below is rating your performance against the tasks in hand. However, because these tests are fairly similar and typical, they are very much 'in the style of', and comparable to, commercially available tests that you might be asked to do. Therefore, your scores should give a good indication as to how well you would do in a 'real' test, with standardised scores. To get a more accurate picture, you would have to complete a commercial test.

These benchmarks should provide you with a good idea of your actual and potential performance.

Summary

In this chapter, you have completed a simple verbal reasoning self assessment test. This will have given you an opportunity to experience something similar to the real thing. We have also used it as an opportunity to explain the difference between raw scores and standardised scores.

Standardised scores compare the results to the spread of scores found in part of the general population. They are usually expressed as:

- Sten scores
- Percentiles or
- Performance bands

Now you have scored your own test, we shall move on to look at what you can do to develop your own skills.

Answers to the test

Section A

1, b; 2, b; 3, a; 4, b; 5, c; 6, d; 7, a; 8, d; 9, a; 10, c; 11, c; 12, b; 13, e; 14, b; 15, d; 16, b; 17, d; 18, e; 19, c; 20, a

Section B

1, c; 2, c; 3, e; 4, d; 5, e; 6, c; 7, e; 8, c; 9, d; 10, d; 11, a; 12, d; 13, b; 14, b; 15, d; 16, c; 17, d; 18, b; 19, a; 20, c; 21, a; 22, b; 23, a; 24, d; 25, c; 26, c; 27, d; 28, c; 29, a; 30, b; 31, c; 32, d; 33, a; 34, c; 35, d; 36, c; 37, b; 38, a; 39, c; 40, b

Section C

1, c; 2, b; 3, c; 4, a; 5, c; 6, a; 7, a; 8, b; 9, c; 10, a; 11, c; 12, a

Where to go next

So far, we have covered quite a lot. You have looked at the nature of verbal reasoning and its relationship to general aptitude and intelligence, the way in which tests are designed, some of the main forms of verbal reasoning test and the way in which they are applied. In the last chapter, you should have completed a test and scored the results to gain more insight into your own abilities in this area.

In this chapter we shall examine how to apply this knowledge to your personal career development. You will find the results of your questionnaire from the last chapter useful. It is of course possible that you may have been disappointed by the results, and we need to ensure that we convert these into practical action. To do this we shall examine:

- What to do with the results
- Identifying learning needs
- Developing verbal reasoning skills
- General advice on personal development opportunities.

What to do with the results

At the beginning of the last chapter, before you completed the simple verbal reasoning test, we asked you to complete a simple table outlining your general cognitive skills as follows:

	above average	average	below average
Verbal ability			
Spelling and Vocabulary			
Word associations			
Critical reasoning			
Numerical ability			
Abstract reasoning			

Obviously, you have no results for Numerical and Abstract reasoning, but how did the rest of your evaluation match the results from the test? You could place a cross in each box to represent your evaluation before the test and then a tick for the results of the test.

If there was a significant difference between the two (either way), it will be worth trying to review the possible reasons for these differences. And by the way, significant underestimation of our abilities is not a good thing. In many ways, it can be more damaging than having an unrealistic view of our abilities.

Let's start to review how we might accurately decide on your abilities based on real facts. Before we start, though, you should remember some simple facts.

1. Most people feel pretty uncomfortable about discussing their general aptitudes and abilities. This is natural.
2. Few people have a balanced profile. They are usually good at some things and poor at others.
3. In terms of employment, what matters most is that your work matches and exploits your natural abilities.

Now having examined your previous self-assessment in the area of verbal reasoning, try to explore the reasons for your judgement, for example:

- How do you know you are right?
- What kind of information or evidence could you use to back up your claim?

Are there any visible outcomes or evidence of your abilities in this area? For example:

- Up to which level was your formal education? Up to 16 (GCSE), Up to 18 (A level, BTEC, GNVQ, Baccalaureate), Higher education (University, HE College) or postgraduate level?
- What are your qualifications? What is the highest level at which you studied language, literature and communications, compared to mathematics or numerical subjects?
- What about your experience and achievements at work? What do they tell you about your abilities and preferences? Do you prefer logic and structure, compared to more abstract topics?
- What are your interests? Do you like to read widely? Do you enjoy doing the Times Crossword? Do you enjoy reading abstract literary essays or poetry?
- Finally, if asked to justify or 'prove' your ability, what evidence could you offer to convince someone (e.g. a potential employer) of your skills in that area?

Now re-visit your original analysis. Do you see any patterns emerging and any explanation for the differences that you may have observed?

	Your Score	Evidence
Verbal ability		
Spelling & vocabulary		
Word associations		
Critical reasoning		
Numerical ability		
Abstract reasoning		

We should emphasise again that the results of this test are nothing like as reliable as a commercial test, but by now you should be beginning to match the results to your own perception of reality.

Identifying learning needs

If your results were disappointing, you need to examine them in more detail to learn from them. After all, knowing that you did not perform well in a particular test achieves nothing unless you can convert this knowledge into improved self awareness at the very least and preferably improved effectiveness. To do this, you need to:

- Examine your test responses more carefully
- Identify your learning needs
- Review possible causes

Examining your test responses

Your total score on any test tells you very little. Your approach to the test and its contribution to the overall score can be very revealing. If you now review your overall approach and the individual responses, you might be able to answer the following questions:

- Did you answer all of the questions? What proportion of questions were left unanswered?
- If you didn't answer all of the questions, what proportion of the questions did you answer correctly?
- Where in the test were most of your incorrect answers? Were they at the beginning, when you were not relaxed, or at the end when you were working in a hurry? Or were they all in one particular section.

If you got most of the questions you answered right, but left too many unanswered, you probably need to work faster next time. If you answered all of the questions, but got many of them wrong, then you should try to work more accurately, even if that means you might have to work more slowly. If the incorrect responses are grouped at the beginning, the end or around a particular section, then you can probably improve the results by trying to reduce your stress and familiarising yourself with questions.

Getting the best results in aptitude tests is often an issue of balancing speed against accuracy. You can certainly improve your performance by getting the balance right for you.

Identifying your learning needs
Once you have eliminated the possibility that your test
technique may have contributed in part to your results, we
are left with an assessment of your verbal reasoning skills,
possibly with some indication of a weaker performance in a
key area such as spelling, grammar or critical reasoning. If
you don't agree with the results, then our advice is to
explore the possibility of undertaking a formal assessment
through an organisation specialising in the provision of
careers advisory support. If you do agree with the results,
you need to ask yourself one important question – *how
important is it to me?*

Of course the answer may be a little more complicated,
because it will involve issues like your personal confidence,
the importance of language in your present job, your career
aspirations and so on. But only you can decide how
important it is, and whether you want to improve your
general language skills in some way.

We should also remind you that aptitude is not the same as
attainment, in other words although you may not have a
natural aptitude for something, you do have the potential to
develop your abilities to a level that may exceed someone
with natural ability.

Review possible causes
As we discussed previously, although the purest form of
verbal reasoning should be relatively free from the
influence of past experience, there is no doubt that past
experience can influence our overall level of confidence
and our overall use of language. Lack of confidence or
even embarrassment about early learning difficulties can

block the progress of many individuals. The removal of unnecessary barriers to confidence can transform the lives of those who may have experienced early learning difficulties at school. There are numerous examples of people who were only diagnosed as suffering from dyslexia (the inability to read words properly due to a physiological condition) later on in life, who thought they were 'thick' but who were able to reach the highest level of intellectual challenge once the cause of their difficulties was identified.

Review the evidence for your level of ability and some of the reasons why you may not perform as well in this area as you would like. If you believe that learning difficulties lie at the heart of any difficulties you experience, you should really discuss the matter with someone who is qualified in this field.

Once you have completed this process, you should have a much clearer idea about the skill areas you wish to improve.

Developing verbal reasoning skills
Although test designers claim that they are measuring aptitude (except where they are specifically trying to measure attainment), there are some things yourself can do to help yourself to develop your skills and facility with words. Verbal reasoning tests essentially test how effectively you think and work in one particular language, here English. The various kinds of item and test are simply trying to assess different aspects of that general mental ability, and clearly a French person would find these tests much more difficult than a native English speaker. It follows therefore

that there are many things you can do to increase your
'word power' or general communication skills, e.g.:

- Widen your vocabulary and
- Use that vocabulary more

Some people have not had their verbal reasoning skills (and
indeed other skill areas) actively assessed or been given
professional feedback since school or college. Here are some
tips of just some of the many things you can do to develop
your skills. However, bear in mind that all of them take
time to achieve results.

Broaden your exposure
- Make a habit of reading a wide variety of reading
  material. Take an interest in other subject areas,
  such as science or the arts.
- Make a deliberate attempt to get to grips with the
  jargon or technical language used by different
  groups you come into contact with.
- Listen carefully to what people are saying and how
  they express themselves. When you listen to a good
  communicator, make a mental note of the words
  and phrases they use, perhaps writing down those
  that particularly strike you.
- As with reading material, try to vary the type of
  material you listen to, such as tapes, radio and
  television shows.

Develop a systematic approach to developing your skills and language ability

- Make a deliberate choice to read more demanding material. Push yourself to read technical or difficult reading matter. At first this will be difficult, but with time you will find that you can read them more easily.
- Make a list of words you frequently misspell and learn how to spell them correctly.
- When you see a new word, look it up in the dictionary. Acquire the habit of underlining words you don't understand and looking them up.
- Make lists of synonyms (words with the same meaning) and antonyms (opposites) by using a dictionary or thesaurus. Start to use the dictionary and thesaurus that are supplied with most modern word processors more actively.
- Write summaries of important bits of text you have read or talks you have listened to.

Become more proactive in communicating with others

- Become a more active reader. Try highlighting key points in text, by underlining words or making notes in the margin. In newspaper or magazine articles, it is sometimes interesting to distinguish facts from the opinions of the writer.
- Ask yourself questions while you are reading or listening to others, e.g. What are they really trying to say? Is that logical? Is that correct?

Make it fun
- Word games and crossword puzzles may not appeal to you, but they are an excellent way to develop your skills. Use your spare time to try out puzzles or games of this kind. If you find them easy, move on to more difficult puzzles. Over time, your general skills will develop significantly.
- Find ways of developing your own tests that you can do anywhere. For example, you can read any text on a train and try to identify the abstract nouns, synonyms or metaphors in the space of a few minutes.

Practise, practise, practise in areas outside your comfort zone
- Involve yourself more in debates, discussions and arguments, possibly joining a debating club or forum. If you feel that this is not necessary, ask yourself whether you tend to limit these to specialist areas in which you feel comfortable.
- Get others to ask you probing questions about important pieces of text you have read.

Ultimately, remember that most people's use of language is profoundly influenced by their level of self confidence. That confidence is of course dependent on their self awareness and belief in their own abilities, supported by regular exposure and continued practice.

If you are interested in trying out example questions that are used in aptitude and ability tests, there are a number of web sites that will provide that opportunity. Psytech

International at www.psytech.co.uk is worth visiting for details, as is www.gmat.org for details of the GMAT test.

General advice on personal development opportunities.

To convert knowledge of your strengths and weaknesses into action and success, you need to do three things:

- Raise your level of awareness
- Identify your key development needs
- Create realistic action plans

Raising your awareness

How often have you discovered something about your performance at work too late to really do anything about it? When people do bring personal development needs to our attention, our response is often we often think '*I always suspected that . . . I wish someone had spoken to me about it earlier*'.

Just as common and significant a barrier to individual and organisational success is a lack of awareness about what people admire you for. Often our reticence to seek feedback is cultural – we feel it's not quite right. But we should always remember that it's difficult to make changes unless we have a very good idea of how others see us. Here is some guidance on how to improve your self awareness.

Increase your sources of feedback

Frequent and regular feedback is the only way to

increase your awareness of your personal skills and qualities effectively. Look for different sources – self assessment tools, your colleagues, your boss, your partner and friends, even perhaps customers. Find ways of asking them what they think, even if it's indirect.

Create your own map

One important problem with psychometric tests is that they use a language which is not yours. Try to develop your own model and understanding of how your personality and intellect work. So instead of verbal reasoning, try to develop your own framework that makes sense to you. You will find this gives you much more control over your life.

Identifying development needs

In the previous section, we suggested ways in which you could identify ways of improving your verbal reasoning skills. Here is some more guidance on how to relate it more to the workplace.

Map your job and environment onto your skills profile

There is no right and wrong when it comes to our own abilities. What is most important is that we exploit our strengths, address our weaknesses and match our working life to our abilities in a way that leads to success and inner happiness. No matter how happy we are in our career, it is always worth comparing where we are and where we want to go to against our personal inventory of skills, e.g.

How well do you suit your current job? Which bits delight you and which do you find frustrating? What is your ideal job? What is the environment like? Who would be your colleagues? How would you work? Why? What does that tell you about your general preferences and abilities?

These are dangerous questions to some people, usually because they feel anxious about the answers and don't want to 'take the lid off'. They are also liberating questions and critical to keeping your life in your hands. Only by identifying what you want out of life, can you begin to match these aspirations to your personal qualities and skills and identify future action points.

Creating a realistic action plan

Assuming that you wish to develop your career, you should use any feedback or self-knowledge to identify priorities for development and an action plan for the future. This is of course the difficult part. Here are some general guidelines for developing your action plan.

- **Add the insight from this book to your overall assessment of your potential**
  What key messages have come from this assessment of verbal reasoning? What are your priorities for the future?
- **Decide how much you want to improve**
  It may seem obvious, but check your own

feelings. Does it really matter? How much? To what lengths are you prepared to go to and why?

- **Link your action plans to your personal aspirations**
  Explore these carefully. Why does It matter? How might your perceived development needs hold you back or frustrate you?
- **Focus on clear, manageable goals**
  Developing general abilities takes a lot of time and patience. Things don't change overnight, so:
  - don't take on too much at once
  - look for short-term objectives with clear benefits for your career that fit longer-term goals
  - make your objectives SMART – specific, measurable, achievable, realistic and time-constrained.
- **Set up processes for on-going support and feedback**
  - Going it alone is always more difficult. Everyone needs the support of others to maximise their potential. Build your own support network, perhaps with colleagues and friends who share the same needs.
  - Look out for people who seem to have the skills you admire. Build in opportunities to work with them or watch them at work.
  - Make sure you get positive, constructive feedback. Negative, non-constructive feedback is always to be avoided.
- **Expect setbacks**
- **Build in your own rewards**

- **Evaluate progress regularly**
  Review, review and review! Be realistic and be
  prepared to adjust your plans if necessary.

And finally ...

Learning about your intellectual abilities such as verbal
reasoning and using this to take control of your personal
development is a difficult but enormously rewarding task. You
will find it more enlightening if you read round the subject and
take the trouble to learn some of the latest techniques and tools
available to assist you. New aptitude tests are being created all
the time and can provide you with an important insight into
your own repertoire of skills and abilities. Keep abreast of
developments and good luck with your plans!

Summary

In this chapter, we have reviewed the results of the self-
assessment test. To get the best from these, you need to be
clear about the factors that contribute to abilities in the area
of verbal reasoning and their relative importance to your
chosen field of work. There are many ways you can increase
your communication skills, but creating effective action
plans to strengthen these skills is not easy. Long-term
success in this area requires you to:

- Raise your level of awareness
- Identify your key development needs
- Create realistic action plans and
- Review your progress constantly

Useful addresses

The British Psychological Society (BPS), 48 Princess Road East, Leicester LE1 7DR. Tel: 0116 254 9568; Fax: 0116 247 0787.

The Institute of Management (IM), Management House, Cottingham Road, Corby, Northants, NN17 1TT. Tel: 01536 204222.

The Institute of Personnel and Development (IPD), IPD House, Camp Road, London SW19 4UX. Tel: 020 8971 9000.

Test suppliers and publishers

Assessment for Selection and Employment, Darville House, 2 Oxford Road East, Windsor, Berks SL4 1DF. Tel: 01753 850333.

Oxford Psychologists Press Ltd, Lambourne House, 311–321 Banbury Road, Oxford, OX2 7JH. Tel: 01865 311353.

The Psychological Corporation, Foots Cray, High Street, Sidcup DA14 5HP

Psytech International Ltd, The Grange, Church Road, Pulloxhill, Beds, MK45 5HE. Tel: 01525 720003. Psytech intend to provide examples of typical test questions on the Web. Visit www.psytech.co.uk for details.

Saville & Holdsworth Ltd, 3 AC Court, High Street, Thames Ditton, Surrey, KT7 0SR. Tel: 020 8398 4170.

The Test Agency, Cray House, Woodlands Road, Henley on Thames, Oxon, RG9 4AE. Tel: 01491 413413.

Further reading

Psychological Testing: Guidance for the User, BPS, Leicester, 1989.

Crozier, A.J.G. *Test Your Personality*, Hodder & Stoughton, 2000.

Avoiding Sex Bias in Selection Testing: Guidance for Employers, Manchester, Equal Opportunities Commission, 1988.

Gael, S. *The Job Analysis Handbook for Business, Industry and Government*, John Wiley and Sons, 1987.

The IPM Code on Psychological Testing, IPD, Wimbledon, 1993.

Lewis, G. *Test Your Numeracy*, Hodder & Stoughton, 2000.

Lewis, G. & Crozier, A.J.G. *Understanding Psychometric Testing in a Week*, Hodder & Stoughton, 1999.

Pearn, M. & Kandola, R. *Job Analysis – A Practical Guide for Managers*, IPM, 1988.

Smith, M. & Robertson, I. *Advances in Selection and Assessment*, John Wiley & Sons, 1993.